- INTRODUCTION OF PHOTOSHOP

INTRODUCTION

Photoshop is a software of image processing. With this you can manipulare your picture, either scanned or otherwise inserted, to such anextent that you would sometimes forget which piture you started off with. But, this is not not the only purpose of the software, you can use it create better looking pictures and arts work with text and other graphics to beat any other similar software in the market, Well first thing first, let us start the software.

STARTING PHOTOSHOP

You can started Photoshop by one the following methods:

Using the Start Menu

1.Click on Start button. The start menu will appear.

2. Click at Programs.

3. Click on Abobe submenu and photoshop submenu.

4. Click on photoshop as shown on the next page.

Using Shortcut

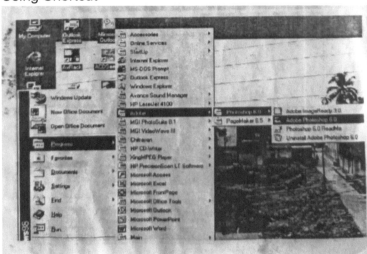

You can use this feature if the icon of the software has been created and is put on the desktop.

1. First located the photoshop shortcut icon.

2. when you find it, position the mouse over the icon and click it to open the software. Using any of the above options you will start the software and get the opening screen first which is shown on the next page.

WHAT'S NEW PHOTOSHOP

Among the various new features the software are;

Preparting Images for the Web

This various of Photoshop offers a numbers of new features that greatly enhance your ability to process images for the Web. By using Photoshop in conjunction with Images Ready, you can produce sophisticated graphics quickly and effectively.

Ersaing areas of layers to transparency

Two new tools-the magic eraser and the background eraser- make it easier for you to erease sections of a layer to transparency. This can be helpful, for example, when you want to delate the background are around a hard-edged object.

Extracting objects from their background

The Extrac commands provides a sophisticated way to isolate a foreground object from its background. Even objects with wispy, intricate or underfinable edges may now be clipped from their backgrounds with a minimum of manual work. You must be working in a layer to use the Extract Command.

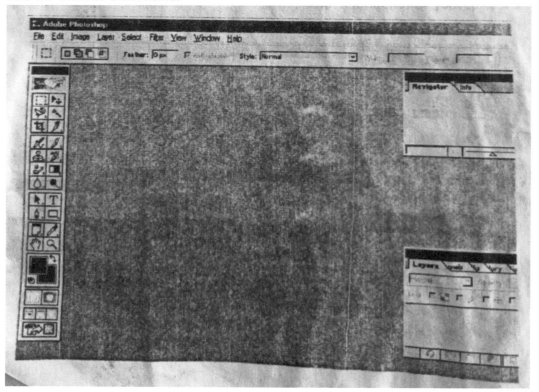

To extract an object, you first use the Extract dialog box to highlight the edges of the object. Then you defined the object's interior and preview the extraction. You can are ready to perform the extraction, photoshop erases the background to transparency, leaving just the extracted object.

Using the art history brush tool

The art history brush tool lets you paint with stylized strokes, using the source data from a specified history starte or snapshot. By experimenting with different paint style, fidelity, size and tolerance otions, you styles.

For a variety of visual effects, experiments with applying filters or filing an image with a soild color before painting with the art history brush tool. For example, set the source history state to the original image, fill the image with white, and use the art history brush tool to paint. Yon can also experiment with custom, non-circular brushes in the Brushes palette.

Creating Multiple image layouts

Photoshop offers new and enhanced features for exporting multiple images automatically as contact sheets, picture packages, and navigable HTML pages.

Adjusting contrast automatically

The new Auto Contrast command lets you adjust the highlights and shadows of an image automatically. The command maps the darkest and lightest pixels in the image to black and white, causing highlights to appear lighter and shadows darker.

When adjusting the contrast, photoshop ignores the first 0.5% range of both the white and black pixels in the image. This clipping of color valuses ensures that white and black values are representative areas of the image's content, rather than extreme pixel values.

To adjust contrast automatically and commands offer new or enhanced options.

Using enhanced tools and commands

A number of photoshop tools and commands offer new of enhanced options.

MENU COMMANDS

One look at these menu commands and you know what is where.

FILE MENU

NEW The New command lets you creats a blank untitled photoshop image. You can also use this commands to create a new image with the exact same pixel dimensions as an image or selection that has been copied copied to the Clip board.

Open It allows you to open an existing file from either the harddisk or other media attached to the computer, floppydrive, CD drive, etc. This also gives rise to a dialog box, from where you can select the file, which you want to open.

Open

It allows you to open a file in another format.

Close

It allows you to close the current phostoshop file.

Save

It saves the current photoshops file.

Save As

It allows you to save the current file under a new name or overwrite the current file.

Save a Copy The Save a copy commands lets you save a copy of the file, leaving the original file intact. You can optionally flatten the file copy and exclude nonimage data or alpha channels.

Save for Web It allow you to save the current file as Web page.

Revert This command is used to restore the most recently saved versions of your file deleting all changes made since the last time you saved it.

Place

This command is used to place the text into the file.

Import This commands is active only if you have the scanner attached to your computer. This will help you in getting the scanned picture into the file.

Export Using this command you can export the selected text of the publication into a document file in the format selected by you.

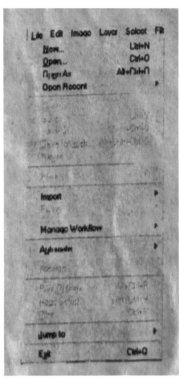

Automate The Automate commands simplify complex tasks by combining them into one or more dialog boxes. photoshop includes the following commands (thrid-party compaines may provided additional command as well):

■Conditional Mode Change the color mode of a documents to the mode you specify, based on the original mode of the document. But recording this commands in an action, you can ensure that any actions that require an image to be in a specific color mode do not generate unwanted error messages.

■Contact Sheet products a series of thumbnail previews on a single sheet from the files in the selected folder. Make sure that the image are closed before applying this command.

■Fit Image fits the current image to width and height you specify, without changing the amount of data in the image.

■Multi-page PDF to PSD convert each page of the PDF DOCUMENT you select to a separate Photoshop file.

File Info Adobe Photoshop supports the information standard developed by the Newspaper Association of America (NAA) and the International Press Telecommunications Council (IPYC) to identify transmitted text and images. This standard in cludes entries and origins. The captions key words, categories, creadits, and origins. The captions and keyword entries can also be searched by some third-party image browsers.

Page Setup You can define here various, options for your new photoshop file

Print This gives rise to a dialog box, where you can set the options for printing the publications.

Jump to This gives you the option to jump to anohter program your choice.

Preferences This command is used to customize your photoshop file according to your preferences.

Color Setting The setting in these dialogs boxes are used for the following:

■To convert image between standard color modes (such as from RGB to CMYK).

■When opening an RGB, GRAYSCALE OR CMYK file to compare the file's color space to the color space defined in the appropriate Setup dialog box. If the two color spaces are not the same, you can convert the file.

■When viewing a file on-screen to covert the file to the monitor;s color space. This only afects the display no the file-photoshop assumes that the file's true color space is the onedefined in the appropriate setur dialog box.

Adobe Online This options will open the Web site of Adobe Corporation to see the latest information on it.

Exit Closes your session with Photoshop

EDIT MENU

Undo/Redo This command is used to reverse the last action taken by you. Howver, you can't undo all the actions. It the action can be reversed, the command read Undo on the Edit menu and names the action such as Undo pasting. If the action can not be reversed the command is off and thus can be read as cannot Undo. After you have do undo, you can redo too if it is allowed.

Cut This command is used to cut the selected text or graphics from your file and keep it available for pasting it later to any other software which supports the clipboard text.

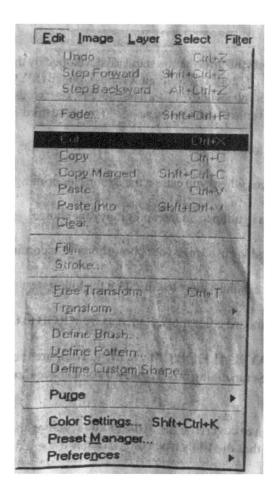

Copy This command is also used to copy the selected text or graphics from your file and keep it available for pasting it later. Only diffierence it has from Cut command is that it leaves the original text as it is where as in the case of cut the original text is lost. When you have more than one publication open you can copy objects between publication without using the Clipboard. Select an object in one publication drag it to position in the other publication window and release the mouse button to create a copy.

Paste This command is used to place the selected text or grapics from clipboard, where the text using the above Cut or Copy command has been kept.

Clear This command is used to delete the current selection from you file without storing it in the Clipboard. This has the same effect as pressing Delete or Backspace.

Fill This commmand is used to fill foreground and background color.

Stroke Photoshop provides a variety of ways to fill a selection or a layer with colors, images or patterns. You can also paint a border around a selectionor a layer using the Stroke command. To increase the contrast between your image and the surrounding work canvas, you can fill the canvas with a specifed colour.

Free Transform When an image is resampled, Adobe Photoshop uses an interpolation method to assign color values to any new pixels based on the color values or existing pixels in the image. The more sophisticated the method, the more quality and detail from the original image are preserved.

Transform

You can use rulers and guides to lay out your work, and you can copy and move selection within an image and between applications. You can also transform objects using specific transformations or using the transform bounding box.

Define Pattern The pattern you define here is repeated as tiles within the selection. Each new pattern replaces the current pattern. If you want to reuse patterns, save a file of swatches for defining patterns. You can also use the patern stamp, tool to paint with a pattern.

Purge The purge command permanently clears from memory the operation stored by the command or buffer, and cannot be undone use the Purge command when inrformation held in memory is so large, Photoshop cannot perform the next operation.

IMAGE MENU

Mode The modes available under Photoshop's this command are: Bitmap; Grayscale; RGB Color, Indexed Color, CMYK Color, Duotone: Lab Color Multichannel

Adjust This command is used to adjust the various color of your image. You will read more about them later.

Duplicate

You can copy an entire image (including all layers, layer masks and channels) into available memory without saving to disk by using the Duplicate command or by dragging and dropping.

Apply Image
 The Apply Image command lets you blend one image's layer and chnnel (the source) with a layer and channel of the active image(the destination).

Calculation The Apply command lets you blend two in dividual channels from one or more source images. You can then apply the results to a new image or to a new channel or selection in the active image. You cannot apply the Calculation command to composite channels.

Image size When preparing image for online distribution (on a Website, for example) it's useful to specify image size in terms of the pixel dimensions affects not only the size of an image on-screen but also its image quality and its printed characteristics either its printed dimensions or its image resoultion.

Canvas Size The canvas size command lets you add or remove work space around the existing image. You can crop an image by decreasing the canvas area. Added canvas appears in the same color or transparency as the background.

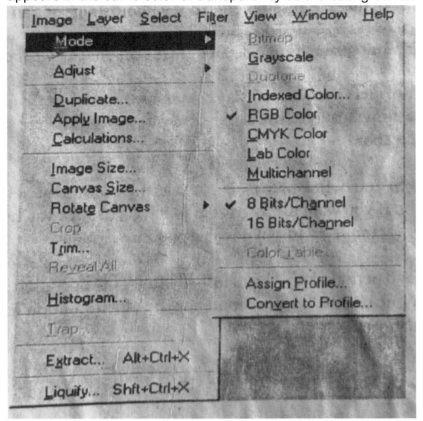

Crop

Photoshop provides two ways to crop an image:

The image > Crop command discards the area outside of a rectangular selection and keeps the same resolution as the original

The crop tool lets you crop an image by dragging over the area you want to keep. The advantage of using the crop tool is that you can rotate and resample the area as you crop.

Rotate Canvas The Rotate Canvas commands let you roate or filp the entire image. It does not work on individual layers or parts of layers, parths, or selection borders.

Histogram The Equalize command redistributes the brightness values of the pixels in an image so that they more evenly repressent the entire range of brightnees levels. When you choose this command, Photoshop finds the brightest and dardkest values in the image so that the darkest value represents black (or as close to it as possible) and the brightest value represents white. Photoshop then at tempts to equalize the brightness-that is to distribute the interme diate pixel value evenly through the grayscale. You might use this command when a scanned image appears darker than the original and you want to balance the value to produce a lighter image. Using the Equalize command lets you see be fore-and-after brightness comparisons.

Trap After you have converted the image to CMYK, you can adjust the color trap. Trap is the overlap needed to ensure that a slight misalignment or movement of the plates while printing does not affect the final appearance of the print job. If any distrinctly differnent colour in your image touch, you may need to over print them slightly to prevent tiny gaps from appearing when the image is printed. This technique is known as trapping is needed and tell you what value to enter in the Trap dialog box.

Extract The Extract command provided a sophisticated way to isolate a foreground object from its background. Even object with wispy, intricate or undefinable edges may now be clipped from their background with a minimum of manual work. You must be working in a layer to use the Extract command. To extract an object, you first use the Extract dialog box to highlight the edges of the object. Then you define the object's interior and preview the extraction as many times as you wish when you are ready to perform the extraction, photoshop erases the background to transparency, leaving just the extracted object.

LAYER MENU

New

This command creates a new layer which can be via Copy or Cut menu.

Duplicate layer This command duplicates the selected layer.

Delete Layer This command delete the selected layer.

Layer Options The layer option let you change a layer's name and opacity and control how the pixels in the layer blend with the layers underneath. It's important to remember that the opacity and blending modes chosen for a specific layer interact with the opacity and mode settings for the tools you use to paint and edit the pixels on the layer.

Adjustment options An adjustment layer lets you experiment with color and tonal adjustments to an image without permanently modifying the pixels in the image. The color and tonal changes reside within the adjustment layer which acts as a veil through which the underlying image layers appear.

When you create an adjustment layer, its effect appearson all the layers below it. This lets you correct multiple layers by marking a single adjustment, rather than making the adjustment to each layer separately.

Effects Adobe photoshop includes a number of automated effects that you can apply to layers, including drop shadow, glows, beve-lling, and embossing. When yoy apply a layer effect, an "f" icon palette. Layer effect are linked to the layer contents. When you move or edit the contents on the layer, the effects are modified correspondingly. Layer effects are especially useful for enhancing type layers.

Type

This command to create type in a layer.

Add Layer Mask In the Layers palette, a layer mask appears as an additional thumbnail to the right of the layer thumbnail. This thumbnail represents the grayscale (alpha) channel created by Adobe Photoshop when you add the layer mask.

Group with Previous In a clipping group, the bottommost layer, or base layer, acts as a mask for the

entire group. For example you might have a shape on one layer, a texture on the overlying layer, and some text on the top most layer. If you define all three as a clipping group, the texture and the text appear only through the shape on the base layer and take on the opacity of the base layer. Note that only successive layers can be included in cliping group. When you create a clipping group, dotted lines appear between the grouped layers in the Layer palette. The name of the base layer in the group is underlined, and the thumb nails for the overlying layer are indented. Applying a blending mode to the base layer determines how the entire clipping group blends with the underlying layers.

Upgroup

This command ungroup the layers grouped to gether by the above command.

Arrange

This command is used for the following:

Bring to Front to mask the layer the topmost layer.

Bring Forward to move the layer one level up in the stacking order.

Send Backward to move the layer one level down in the stacking order.

Send to Back to make the layer the bottom most layer in the image (except for the background)

Align Linked

This command is usd for the following:

To align a single layer to a selection, make the layer active.

To align multiple layers to a selection or to the active layer, link together twoor more layers.

To distribute multiple layers, link together three or more layers.
Top to align the topmost pixel on the linked or the top most edge of the selection border

Vertical Centre to align the vertical centermost pixel on the linked layers to the vertical centermost pixel on the active layer or the vertical centre of the selection border.

Bottom to align the bottommost pixel on the linked layers to the bottommost pixel on the active layer or the bottommost edge of the selection border.

Left to align the leftmost pixel on the linked layers to the leftmost pixel on the active layer or the leftmost edge of the selection border.

Horizontal Center to align the horizontal centermost pixel on the linked layers to the horizontal

centermost pixel on the active layer or the horizontal center of the selection border.

Right to align the rightmost pixel on the linked layers to the rightmost pixel on the active layer or the rightmost edge of the selection border.

Merge Layers

This command is used for merging more than one layer.

Merge Visible

This command makes sure that the merged layers are visible.

Flatten Image In a flattened image, all visible layers are merged into the background, greatly reducing file size. Flattening an image discards all hidden layers and fill the remaining trans parent areas with whit. In most cases, you won't want to flatten a file until you have finished editing individual layers.

Matting When you move or paste an anti-aliased selection, some of the pixels surroundingt the selection border are include with the selection. This can result in a fringe or halo around the edges of the paste selection. These three Matting commmand let you edit these undwanted edge pixels:

Defrige replaces the colour of any fringe pixels with the colors of nearby pixels containing pure colors (those without background colour). For example, if you select a yellow object on a blue background and then move the selection, some of the blue background is selected and moved with the object. Defringe replaces the blue pixels with yellow ones.

☐ Remove Block Matte ann Romove White Matter are useful when you want to paste a selection anti-aliased against a white or black background into a different background. For example, anti-aliased black text on a white background has gray pixels at the edges, which are visible against a colored background.

SELECT MENU

All This command selects all the items on the screen.

Deselect This command deselects the items already selected.

Reselect You can reselect the items deselect above.

Color Range The Color Range command select a specified color or color subset within an existing selection or an entire image. If you want to replace a selection, be sure to deselect everything before applying this command.

Feather You can define fathering for the marquee, lasso, polygon lasso, or magnetic lasso tool as you use the tool, or you can add feathering to an existing Selection. Feathering eflect become apparent when you move, cut, or copy the selection.

Modify You can use the following Select command to increase or decrease the pixels in an existing selection:

п

Modify to expand or contract a selection by specified number of pixels.

п

Grow and Similar to expand a selection to include areas similar in color.

п

Smooth to clean up any stray pixels left inside out side a color based selection.

Grow

Grow and Similar command are used to expand selection to include areas similar in color.

Transform Selection The Free Transform command lets you use Scale, Rotate, Skew, Distort, and Perspective command without having to select them from the menu. To access the various trans foramtion modes, you use different shortcut keys as you drag the handles of the transform bounding box.

Load Selection When you have finished modifying an alpha channel or simply want to use a previously saved selection, you can load the selection into the image.

Save Selection You create a new alpha channel as a mask. For example, you can create a gradient fill in a blank channel, and then use it as mask. Or you can save selection to either a new or existing channel.

Fit on Screen

These options scale both the view and the win dows size to match the monitor size.

Actual Pixels

This command displays the image at 100%

Print Size

The magnification of the image is adjustment to display its approxi mate printed size, as specified in the Print Size section of the Image Size dialog box.

Show Rules

Show or hides rules on the screen.

Hide Guides

This command is selectected all guides whether margin, column or ruler exert presure on any tool, text or graphic when they are within short range of the guides.

Lock Guides

This command locks all the column and ruler guides so that you cannot moves them accidentally.

Clear Guides

This command clears all guides from the screen.

Show Grid

This command shows all the grids on the screen.

Snap To Grid

When this command is selected all grids exert pressure on any tool, text or graphic when they are within short range of the grids.

WINDOW MENU

Cascade

This command opens another window of the curent image.

Tile

Using this command you can see on the screen more than one image.

Arrange Icon

This command arranges icons on the screen.

Close All

This command close all the open windows on the screen.

Hide Tools

Hides/Shows the tools dialog box on the screen.

Hide Navigator

Hid/Shows the Navigator dialog box on the screen.

Various options available under this command are: Colored Pencil, Cutout, Dry Brush, Film Grain, Fresco, Neon Glow, Paint Daubs, Palette Knife, Plastic Wrap, poster Edges, Rough Pas tels, Smudge Stick, Sponge, Underpainting and Watercolor.

Soften a selection or an image. Blur filters are useful for retouching.

They smooth transitions by averaging the pixels next to the hard edges of defined lines and shaded areas in an image. Various options available under this command are: Blur, Blur more, Gaussain Blur, Motion Blur, Radial Blur, Smart Blur.

okes

Like the Artistic filters, the Brush strokes filters give a painterly or fine-arts look using different brush and inkstroke effects. Some of the filters add grain, paint, noise, edge detail, or texture to an image for a pointillist effect. Various option available under this command are:

accented Edges, Angled, Strokes, Crosshatch, Dark Strokes, Ink Out lines, Spatter, Sprayed Stroke and Sumie:

Geometrically distort an image, creating 3-D or other re shaping effects, Note that these filters can be very memory intensive. This command has the following option: Diffuse Glow, Displace, Glass, Ocean Ripple, Pinch, Polar coordinates, Ripple, Shear, Spherize, Twirl, Wave and ZigZag.

Add or remove noise, or pixels with randomly distributed color levels.

This helps to blend a selection into the surrounding pixels. Noise filters can create unusual textures or remove problem areas, such as dust and scratches, from an image. The Add Noise filter can be used to readuce banding in feathered selection or graduated fill or to Despeckle, Dust & scratches and Median.

Sharply define a selection by clumping pixels of similar color values in cells. This command has following option: color Halftone, crystallize, Facet, Fragment, Mezzotint, Mosaic and Pointillize.

Create 3-D shapes, cloud patterns, refraction patterns, and simulated light reflection in an image. You can also manipulate objects in 3-D space, create 3-D object (cubes, spheres, and cylinders), and create tex ture fills from grayscale files to produce 3-D like effect for lighting. This command has the following option: 3D Transform, Clouds, Differ ence Clouds, Lens Flare, Lighting Effects and Tex ture Fill.

Focus blurry images by increasing the contrast of adjacent pixels. They include the Sharpen Edges and Unsharp mask filters, which find and sharpen areas where significant color changes occur (such as at the edges). The Unsharp mask filter is commonly used for high-end color correc-tion. this command has the following option: sharpen, Sharpen Edges, Sharpen More and Unsharp Mask.

Add texture to images, often for a 3-D effect. The filters also are useful for creating a fine arts or hand-drawn look. Many of the sketch filters use the foreground and background color as they redraw the image. Vari ous options under this command are: Bas Relief, Chalk &

Charcoal, Char coal, Chrome, Conte Crayon, Graphic Pen Half tone Pattern, Note Paper, Photocopy, Plaster, Reticulation, Stamp. Torn Edges and Water Paper.

Produce a painted or impressionistic effect on a selection by displacing pixels and by finding and heightening contrast in an image. After using filters like Find Edges and Trace Contour That high light edges, you can apply the Invert command to outline the edges of a color image with colored lines or to outline the edges of a gray image with white lines. Various option under this command are: Deffuse, Emboss, Extrude, Find Edges, Glowing Edges, Solarize, Tiles, Trace Contour and Wind.

Texture

Give images the appearance of depth or sub stance, or add a organic look. Various option under this command are: Craquelure, Grain, Mo saic Tiles, Patchwork, Stained Glass and Texturizer.

Video

Include the NTSC (National Television Standards Committee) Colors filter, which restricts the gamut of colors to those acceptable for televistion reproduction and the De-Interlace filter, which smooth mov ing image captured on video. This command has the following option: De-Interlace and NTSC Colors.

Other

Let you create your own filters, use filters to modify masks, offset a selection within an image, and make quick color adjustment. This com mand has the following option: custom, DitherBox, High Pass, Maxi-mum, Minimum and offset.

Digimarc

Embed a digitial watermark into an image to store copyright informa-tion. This command has the following option: Embed Watermark and Read watermark.

VIEW MENU

New View

This command opens another view of the same image.

Preview

For accurate color printing it is essential to calibrate your monitor and the Adobe Photoshop program for the various factors that affect the printed output. This command helps in doing the same.

Gamut

warning The gamut is the range of colors that can be displayed or printed in a color system. A color that can be displayed in RGB or HSB models may be out-of-gamut, and therefor unprintable, for your CMYK setting. Photoshop automatically brings all color into gamut when you convert an image to CMYK. But you might want to identify the out-of-gamut colors in image or correct them manually before converting to CMYK.

Zoom In

Select the zoom tool, and click the area you want to magnify: Each click magnifies the image to the next present percentage, centering the dis play around the ponit you click. At maximum magnification, the centre of the zoom tool appears empty.

Zoom out

Select the zoom tool. Hold down Alt (Windows or Option (Mac OS) to activate the zoom-out tool anc click the area of the image you want to reduce. Each click reduce the view to the previous preset percentage.

Fit on Screen

These options scale both the iew and the win dows size to match the monitor size

Actual Pixels

Print Size

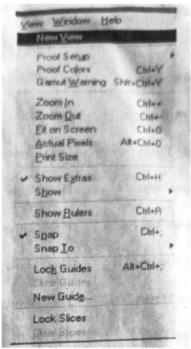

This command displays the image at 100%

The magnification of the image is adjustment to display its approximate printed size, as specified in the Print Size section of the Image Size dialog box.

View Window

Help

New View

Proof Setup

Proof Colors

Chi-Y

Gamut Warming

Shit-Orl-Y

Zoom in

Zoom Qu

C

Eit on Screen

Actual Pixels

AR-Chl-O

Print Size

Show Extras

Show

CM-H

Show Bulers

Cal-R

✓Snap

Chi

Snap To

Lock Guides

Ar+Chl

New Guide.

Lock Slices

Show Rules

Show or hides rules on the screen.

Hide Guides

This command is selectected all guides whether margin, they are within short range of the guides. column or ruler exert presure on any tool, text or graphic when

Lock Guides

This command locks all the column and ruler guides so that you cannot moves them acciden tally.

Clear Guides

This command clears all guides from the screen.

Show Grid

Snap To Grid

WINDOW MENU

Cascade

Tile

Arrange Icon

Close All

Hide Tools

This command shows all the grids on the screen.

When this command is selected all grids exert pressure on any tool, text or graphic when they are within short range of the grids.

This command opens another window of the curent image.

Using this command you can see on the screen more than one image.

This command arranges icons on the screen.

This command close all the open windows on the screen.

Hides/Shows the tools dialog box on the screen.

Hide Navigator

Show Info

Hid/Shows the Navigator dialog box on the screen.

Hide/Shows the Info dialog box on the screen.

Show Options

Hide/Shows the options dialog box on the screen.

Hide Colour

Hide/Shows the Color dialog box on the screen.

Show Swatches

Hide/Shows the Swatches dialog box on the screen.

Show Brushes

Hide/Shows the Brushes dialog box on the screen.

Hide Layers

Hide/Shows the Layers dialog box on the screen.

Show Paths

Hide/Shows the Layers dialog box on the screen.

Show History

Hide/shows the History dialog box.

Show Actions

Hide/Shows the actions dialog box on the screen.

Hide Status Bar

Hide/Shows the status bar on the screen.

Open Files

This command shows the open files.

Help Menu

This menu has the various options which help you in case you

Hide Navigator

Hid/Shows the Navigator dialog box on the screen.

Show Info

Hide/Shows the Info dialog box on the screen.

Show Options

Hide/Shows the options dialog box on the screen.

Hide Colour

Hide/Shows the Color dialog box on the screen.

Show Swatches

Hide/Shows the Swatches dialog box on the screen.

Show Brushes

Hide/Shows the Brushes dialog box on the screen.

Hide Layers

Hide/Shows the Layers dialog box on the screen.

Show Paths

Hide/Shows the Layers dialog box on the screen.

Show History

Hide/shows the History dialog box.

Show Actions

Hide/Shows the actions dialog box on the screen.

Hide Status Bar

Hide/Shows the status bar on the screen.

Open Files

This command shows the open files.

Help Menu

This menu has the various options which help you in case you want to know more about any commnad.

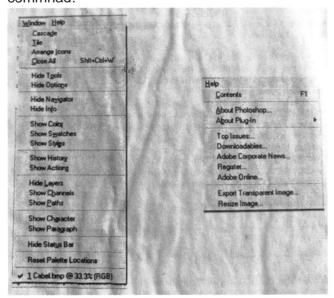

USING SELECTION TOOLS

INTRODUCTION

A picture can be selected in Photoshop by using various tools which are available with the software. It is so because teh selection various from time to time. There are tools which would select the whole picture or a pixel of a picture.

✓ MARQUEES-RECTANGLE AND OVAL

These tools are available on the top of the toolbar. The rectrangular tool is available on the toolbox. if pressed it gives rise to the various tools available under it.

Click the Marquee tool in the toolbox. Move the tool over the blank canvas of your file and see the result, You can create a rectangular marquee with it as shown on the next page.

If you press and hold shift key after you have made your first selection before you click again, you can make additional selections. This shift key can also help you draw a per-fectly round circle or can even square. Press shift as drag the shape, and Photoshop will constrain the shape as you draw it.

LASSO TOOL

These tools are used when you have to select irregular shapes. Using the Lasso tool to select an object requires a steady hand and good-eye coordination, as well as a clean mouse and mousepad or trackball.

To select the Lasso tool, do the following:

1. Click mouse to select the Lasso tool from the toolbox.

2. Click and drag the tool around the piece of the image you want to select.

3. Release the mouse button to complete your selection.

POLYGON LASSO TOOL

This tool also behaves in much the same way as the regular Lasso tool. The difference is

as its name implies, it can make irregular geometric selection on the image.

To selection the Polygon Lasso tool, do the following:

1. Click mouse to select the Lasso tool from the toolbox. Keep it click till the rollout

menu appears. 2. From this menu select teh Polygon Lasso tool.

3. Instead of a box selection as done in the previous case, here the selection can be done in steps.

4. Click once on the image from Where you want to start, Move the cursor to the next point to see the line following you.Click here to make the line.

5. Again move the mouse to move further and thus keep selecting the various point on the image which would form the part of the selection.

6. Move around till you reach the first, i.e, the stating point of the tool.

7. Click here to end the selection.

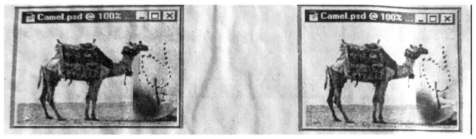

MAGETIC LASSO TOOL

This tool is one of the most used Lasso tool. As your drag around any shape with a reasonably well-defined edge, it snaps to the edge. It is most effective on irregular ob-jects thatstand out from the background.

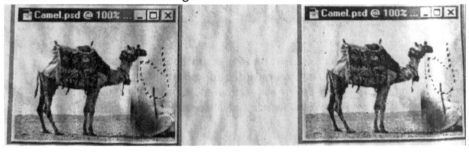

MAGIC WAND TOOL

This tool is little different from the other selection tools. This Magic Wand selects pixels some what differently, it selects them based on color values. This enables you to cut foreground objects, out of the background.

Its tolerance can be set in the Options palette. Tolerance here refers to the Magic Wand's sensitivity to colour differences.

FEATHER TOOL

This tool helps you make selections with fussy, feathered edges rather than hard ones. It is very helpful when you want to select an object from one picture and paste it into another one, because it adds a slight blur that helps to blend it.

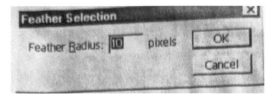

To make the feathered selection do the following:

1. Choose an appropriate Selection tool and use it to select a piece of picture or an object with the picture.

2. Choose Select, Feather to open the dialog box.

3. Enter an amount in the windows. Start with 5 and increased or decreased until the selection looks right to you.

CUTTING AND COPYING TOOLS

These command here are indetical to teh ones available in the other software and work on teh similar lines too. You will find them all in the Edit menu Cut Copy and Paste.

Cutting copying and pasting allow you to borrow from one picture to add to another. You can even used the common keyboard shortcuts of the same as:

Cut-Ctrl+X

Copy-Ctrl+C

Past-Ctrl+V

CROPPING TOOL

This tool helps you in getting rid of unwanted parts of the picture. It forms part of the marquee tools submenu. You can also crop by marking a selection with the rectangular

marquee and then using the

menu command image Crop to crop the image.

If another cropping you realize that whatever you have done is not correct. Just unod it and you are back to the original.

USING PAINTBRUSHES AND ART TOOLS

INTRODUCTION

Photoshop comes with lots of art tools which allow you to create an artwork on the screen itself right from the scratch.

Various available tools are:

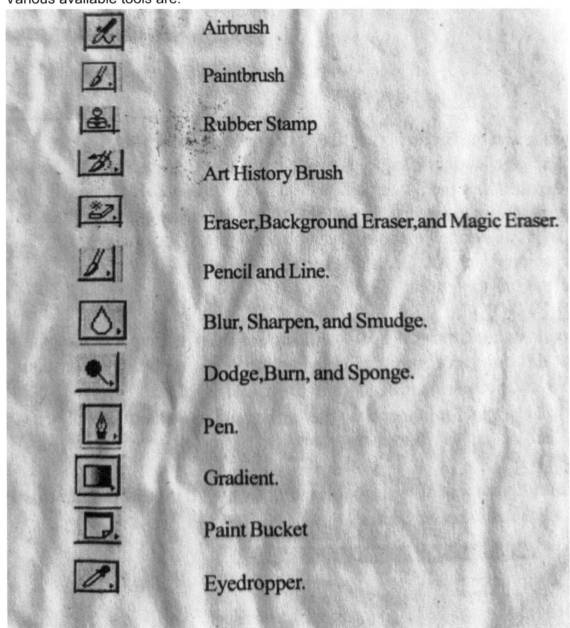

Airbrush

Paintbrush

Rubber Stamp

Art History Brush

Eraser,Background Eraser,and Magic Eraser.

Pencil and Line.

Blur, Sharpen, and Smudge.

Dodge,Burn, and Sponge.

Pen.

Gradient.

Paint Bucket

Eyedropper.

UNDERSTANDING BRUSHES:

There are various types of brushes available under Photoshop. You can get a brush dialog box, as shown below, by just clicking at Windows menu and clicking at Show brushes.

Click one of the brush shapes to select it. The size shape you see are the size and shape of the brush. The ones with numbers indicates the diameter of the brush in pixels. A brush can be of a maximum of 14 inches. You can also select brush option dialog box for more brush options.

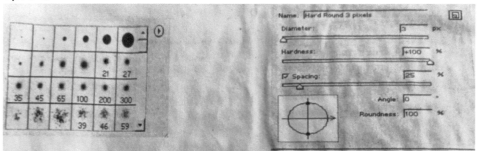

Double click a brush and the Brush option dialog appears, as shown below. You can change here the diameter, hardness, angle, and roundedness of the brushes.

Hardness of the brushes how the brush paint would be at the edges. If spacing is left unselected, the speed of your mouse movement determines the spacing discrete drops of paint. You can also play around with the angle and Roundness of the brushes. You can also save a brush option which you feel is best suitable to you.

Let us now try out various tools.

THE AIRBRUSH TOOL

This tool sprays paint on the canvas. As you would notice from its shape, its like paint being sprayed from the spray paint cannister through a nozzle. The Airbrush applies paint with diffused edges, and you can control how fast the paint is applied. If you hold the brush at a spot for longer time the darker and more saturated the color

becomes there as seen on the perviouse page.

PAINTBRUSH TOOL

This tool is the most important of all brush tools in Photoshop. It is quite similar to the Airbrush but here teh paint is applied quite evenly.

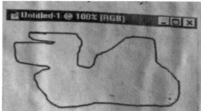

HISTORY BRUSH TOOL

This tool is very useful when you are making change in an image arn are not sure exactly how much change to make or where to make it. it enables you to selectively put back part of the picture in which you are making changes by selecting a brush size and painting of the new image with the old one.

The Art History Brush tool, which is new to Photoshop 5.5, paints with a various of stylized strokes but, like the history Brush, it uses the source data from a specified history state of snapshot.

To apply the Art History Brush do the following:

1. On the History palette, click the left column of the state you want to be as the source for the Art History Brush tool. You will see a brush icon next to the thumbnail image, as shown on the here.

2. Choose the Art History Brush and-double-click it to open its Options paletta. The Art History Brush tool is grouped with the History Brush tool in the toolbox.

3. Set the Blending mode to normal. Set the opacity to 75%. You can change it as you see the effect.

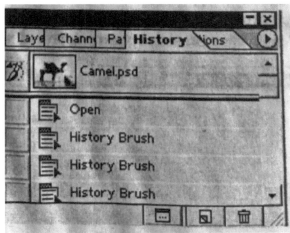

4. Choose an option from the Paint Style menu, located to the left of the Fidelity setting in the opitons palette. This choice controls the shape of the paint stroke.

5. Enter a value for Fidelity or drag the slider to control how much the paint color deviates from the color in the source. The lower the fidelity the more the color will vary from the source.

6. For Area, enter a value to specify the area covered by the paint strokes Lager sizes mean larger areas covered and more paint strokes.

7. Enter a Tolerance value or drag the slider to limit the regions where paint stoke can be applied. A low tolerance limits paint stroke to areas that differ significantaly from the colour in the source.

8. Select a brush shape and start painting.

ERASER TOOLS

The next set of tools are the Eraser tools. Basides Eraser, you have Background Erases and Magic Erase tools too. These eraser make it easier for you to section of a layer to transparency.

The Background Eraser tool lets you eraser pixels on a layer to transparency as your drag. The Magic Eraser tool automatically eraser all similar pixels to transparency. You can choose to eraser contiguous pixels only or all similar pixels on the current layer.

PENCIL TOOL

This tool works like the Painbrush tool, except that it can only create hard-edges lines. These lines do not fade at the edges as paintbrush lines do.

You can set the diameter of your Pencil in the Brushes option palette, but hardness is not an option.

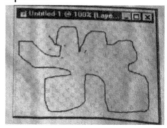

UNDERSTANDING COLOURS

INDRODUCTION

Colour are everywhere around us. But how does one colour differ from another. There are a number of colour libraies and each one of them have different shade. There is so much to colour that it may need one book to study each one of the. Let us concentrate on what is available under Photoshop.

We would be talking about 4 different type of colour modes:

RGB(Red, Green and Blue)

CYMK(Cyan, Yellow, Magenta and Black)

HSB (Hue, Saturation and Brightness)

CIE Lab

Let us study them one by one.

RGB MODEL

This is made up of three primary colours, i.e. Red, Green and Blue, Most of the colours are the mixture of all these. For example a pure Red will be 255, Maximum for a colour, of Red an 0 of Green and Blue each,. While the white would be 255 of each and Black would be 0 of each.

The next page shows all the three options.

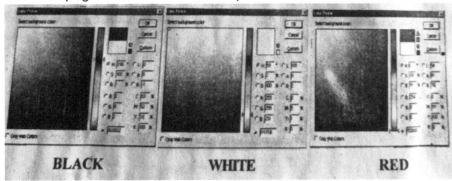

CYMK MODEL

As said earler CYMK stands for cyan, Yellow, Magenta and Black. These 4 also make a set of combinations to from different colours. Here you have to add them according to percentage of each one of them. This of colours are used by the high-end laser printers and are mostly used by commercial printers.

Few example of CMYK colour combinations are given below.

HSB MODEL

This is another colour combination where H stand for Hue, S for Saturation and B for Brightness. Here Hue is the basic colour from the colour wheel which is expressed in terms of degrees from 0 to 360. It reprewents the position of the colour on the colour wheel.

Saturation is the strength of the colour. It is measured in percentage of colour minus the amount of gray in it. Brightness is also measured in terms of percentage. It varies from 0 where it is black and to 100 where it is white.

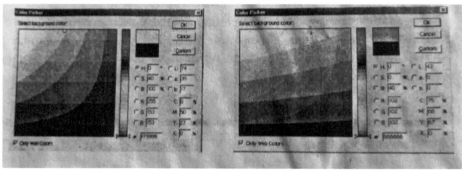

CIE LAB

Photoshop uses the CIE mode, because its gamut is so broad, to convert from one colour model to another

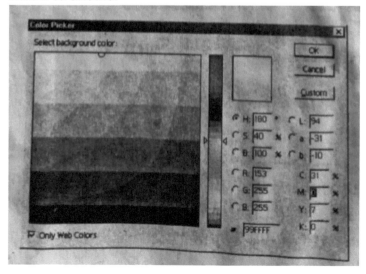

WORKING MODELS

You would be working in RGB modes mostly in Photoshop. The differences between modes and models is simple. The models are methods of defining colour. Modes are methods of working with colour based on the models. There are modes for black and white too like, Grayscale and Limited Colour work.

BITMAP AND GRYSCALE MODE

The Bitmap mode uses only two colour values to display images-black and white, while the Grayscale mode offers 256 shades of gray that range from white to black.

Whenever a picture is printed in black and white or Grayscale, for instance as part of a newsletter or borchure, it makes sense for you to work on it in Grayscale mode. To convert a color image to Grayscale simple choose Image; Mode, Grayscale. You will asked for permission to discard the colour information. Clock Ok to confirm, and pic-ture is converted to grays.

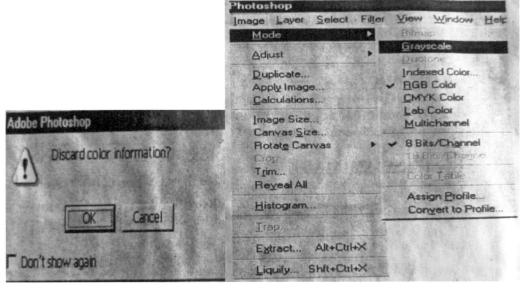

INDEXED COLOURS

Indexed colour is a palette or rather a collection of paletters-256 to be exact. With this mode you do not like any of the palettes Photoshop supplies you can build your own. This type of colours are perfact for World Wide Web.

Dithering means that certain colours are combined, that is adjacent pixels are interspersed, visually blending on screen to create a new colour although they retain their original colour-or the closest index equivalent-when viewed at a large magnification.

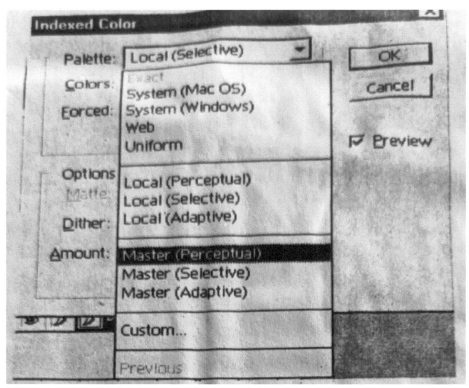

USING TRANSFORMATIONS

INTRODUCTION

There will be times when you need to make an object bigger or smaller as you copy it from one picture to another. You may to straighten a titled horizon, or even stand some-thing upright. You may need to make someone faces left intead of him facting right.

RESIZING AN IMAGE

For this we use the Image Size dialog box, as shown below. You can see the pixel

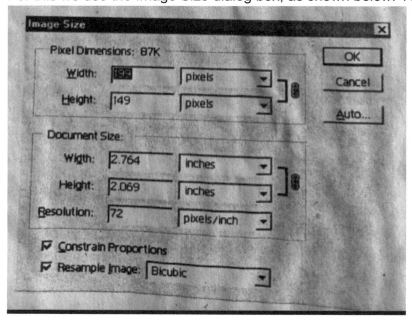

dimensions in pixels or percentage. You can also see the image print size in inches, centimeters, point, picas, or columns: percentage can also be found using the pop-up menus.

When the dialog box is first opened, all the setting are to the 100% of the image. You can change this percentage to enlarge or reduce the image. But, the easiest way to do it to take the help of Constrain Properties.

RESIZING A CANVAS

Resizing the canvas larger gives you extra work space around the image, instead of changing the size of the image. It is so because resizing uses teh current background colour to fill in the space, be sure it is a colour you want. To resize the canvas, open the Image, Canvas size dialog box, as shown below, to specify the height and surement systems you prefer on the pop-up menu. The new file size is caculated immediately and displayed.

The anchor at the bottom is used to determine where the image will be placed within the canvas, Click in the middle, to centre the image on the enlarged canvas or in any of the other boxes to place it relative to the increased canvas area.

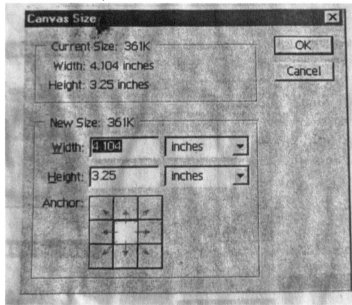

RESIZING A SELECTION

You can also resize a selected object. To do so, first select the object or a piece of an image to be resized. Use whichever Selection tool is most covenient. With the Selection Marquee active, choose Edit, Transform, Scale. This places a window that look like the cropping window around your selection object. Drag on any of the corner handles on the box to change the size of the image while holding down the Shift key to maintain its proportions. If you drag on the side handles of the box, you will stretch the selection's height or width accordingly.

The various steps are shown here and on the next few pages.

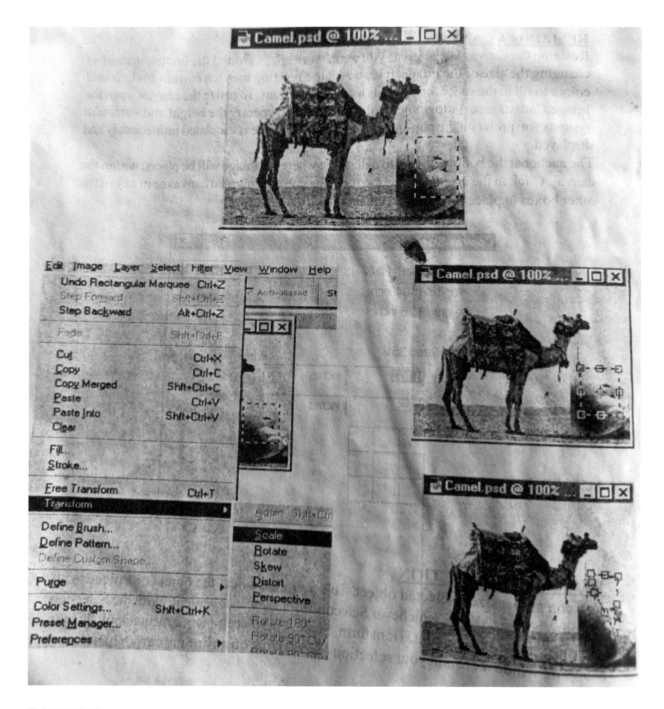

ROTATING

There are many reasons why you might want to need to rate an image. If you have a scanned picture or a digital camera image that should be vertical but opens as a horizontally-oriented picture, rotating it at 90 degrees corrects teh problem.

If the above picture of Zebra is rotated at 180 degrees, it will give you the picute as shown on the next page.

Under the Image menu and Rotate Canvas submenu, you have options like 90 degrees clockwise, 180 degrees or counterclockwise (CCW)

If you are however, keen to rotate the picture according to teh degrees of your choice you can do so by choosing the Arbitrary dialog box also available under the same submenu.

Result of this 30 degrees rotation can be seen on the next page

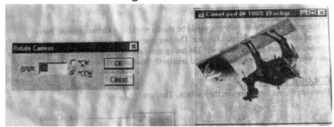

NUMERIC TRANSFORMATIONS

This type of transformations is for those who consider themselves to be good as calcu-lation. You have to do all the calculations. You have to do all the calculations and fill up the spaces according to your guess work and then click OK.

The Numeric Transformation box, shown on the next page, can be obtained from the Image menu and Transformation submenu.

Here you can entre numeric values for the position scale, skew and rotaion. However, you cannot see them in advance, in the form of a preview.

Luckity, we have the option of Undo. So apply it and if you do not like it, Undo it.

USING PAINTS:

INTRODUCTION

While working in Photoshop you would be mostly working with two colours: Fore-ground colour and Background colour. The foreground is the colour where all your brushes and pens, pencil will work. The background colour is the colour photoshop uses when you erase or delete a selected area on the background layer.

COLOUR TOOLS

There are 4 tools for colours on the toolbox,. They are:

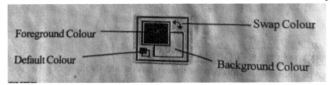

COLOUR PICKER

Colour picker dialog box, which we had seen in the earlier chapter, lets you select a foreground or background colour in any several ways. You can click the colour spectrum

A colour usually a mixture of few colour. You ass some Red, some Blue and may be some yellow and Black to make certain colour. There is no rule governing this. You can mix any quantity so any colour and make the colour which suits you. Few colour samples are shown below:

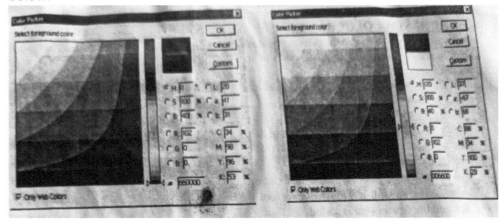

THE COLOUR PALETTE

It is not that you have to work with Colour Picker only. You have Paletters too, which are as good but not that much detailed. You can leave it open on the desktop, so you can change colour without having to go through all the fuss of clicking a swatch in the toolbox, finding the colour, and then OK your choice.

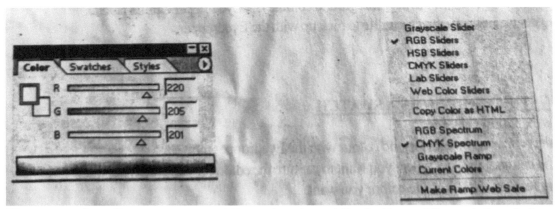

The menu also allows you to reset the colour bar at the bottom of the palette window, according to the colour models with which you are working. By clicking at the right button on the right top of the palette. If you click Make Ramp web Safe, the only colour displayed on the colour baz will be the 216 colours that all current Web browsers can display.

THE SWATCHES PALETTE

The Swatch palette works like a box of watercolours of a child on the screen. You simply dip your brush in any colour and painting with it, To choose a foreground colour, simply click the one you want. To choose a background colour, prsss Option+click to select the colour you want to use.

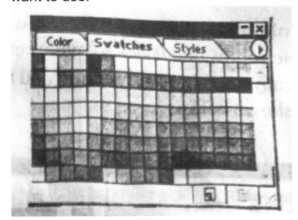

ADDING NEW COLOURS

For adding a new colour to the palette, you do the following:

1. Click the foreground colour swatch in the toolbox.

2. Use the colour Picker to select the desired colour and click OK.

3. Open the Swatches palette.

4. Using the tab in teh lower-right corner of th3e Swatches plaette, drag the window out so that it

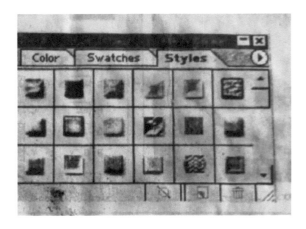

resembles the one shown here.

5. Move your cursor into the space the existing swatches. It changes into the Paint Bucker tool.

6. Click and the new colour is added.

7. If you press, Shift, you can add the new colour anywhere you like, replacing whatever swatch you click.

314

THE EYEDROPPER TOOL

The eyedropper tool is extremely helpful, especially when you are retouching a picture and need to duplicate the colours in it. Click it on any spot in the image and colour underneath its tip become the new foreground colour. The Eyedropper Option palette, lets you decide how much of a sample to pick up with the Eyedropper.

SAVING FOREGROUND AS A SWATCH

To do this the following steps:

1. Click the following or background colour with the Eyedropper tool.

2. Click the image at the spot where you want to capture the colour. If you are saving the background colour, Alt+click the colour you want.

3. Open the Swatches palette, if it is not already open. Put the Eyedrop per on any empty (gray) space in the Swatch palette. It turns into a Paint Bucket.

4.Click once to put a swatch of the selected colour into the palette.

5. Choose Save Swatches from the palett's pull-out menu.

6. Follow the usual procedure to name your Swatch file, and save it in

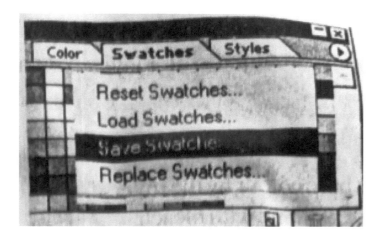

BLENDING MODE

When you place a second brush full of paint over one that has already there, different thing happen, depending on the colour of the paint you are applying. In Photoshop, you can control all these factors by applying what is called Blending modes. Following are the option which you can choose from the various painbrush option under its menu.

NORMAL

This is the default mode. The blend colour replace the base colour.

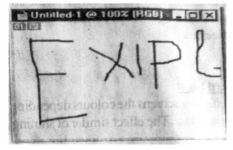

DISSOLVE

A radom number of pixels is changed to become the blend colour. Gives a spattered or dry brush effect.

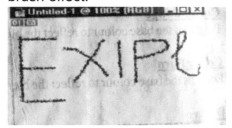

Multiply

It multiplies the base colour by blend colour, giving you a darker colour. The effect is like drawing over the picture with a magic marker.

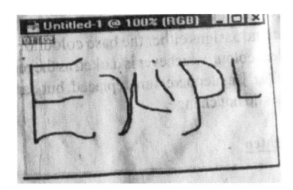

Behind

Works only transparent parts of a layer. You appear to be painting on the back of a sheet.

Screen

It multiples the base colour by the inverse of the blend colour, giving you lighter colour. The effect is like painting with bleach.

Overlay

Either multiple or screen, depending on the base colour. Preserves the highlights and shadow of the base colour.
Soft Light

Darkness or lightness depending on the blend colour. The effect is said to be simi-lar to shining a diffused spotlight on the im-age. With a light blend colour, it has very little effect.

Multiple or screens the colours depending on the colour. The effect similar ot shining a harsh spotlight on the image.

Colour Dodge

Brightens the base colour to reflect the blend colour.

Colour Burn

Darkens the base colour to reflect the blend colour.
Darken

Evaluates the colour information in each chan-nel and assigns either the base colour or the blend colour, whichever is darket, as the result colour. Lighter pixels are replaced, but darker ones do not change.

Lighten

Evaluates the colour information in each channel and assigns either the base colour or the blend colour, whichever is lighter, as the result colour. Darker pixels are replaced, but lighter ones do change. This is the exact opposite of Darken.

Difference

Compares the brightness values in base and blend, and subtracts teh lighter from the brighter.

Hue

Gives you a result combining the luminance and saturation of the base colour and the hue of the blend colour.

Saturation

It gives you a colour with the Luminance and hue of the base colour and the saturation of blend colour. Unless you reduce the saturation of the blend colour significantly,nothing shows

Colour

Retains the luminance of the base colour with the hue and saturation of the blend colour. Useful for colouring monochrome inages as it retains the gray levels.

Luminosity

Give result colour with the hue and saturation of the base colour and the luminance of the blend colour. Opposite effect Colour Blend mode.

Similar to the Difference mode, but with a softer effect.
SMUDGES

When you blend two or more colours, it is called Smudging. You can do this in more than one way. The smudge tool looks like a finger. It is the same toolbox compart-ment with the Blur and Sharpen tools. The Smudge tool picks up colour from wherever you start to drag it and moves it in the direction which you drag. Following are the smudges at 100%, 50% and 25%.

You can set the smudge option from the Smudge Tool Option dialog box.

The Blending modes are on a pulldown menu. This tool does not give all the Blending

mode option but you can choose, aside from normal, as show here, Darken, Lighten, Hue, Saturation, Colour, or Luminosity. Of these Darken and Lighten modes are mostly used.

FOCUS TOOLS

These tools are: Blur and Sharpen. They can be used to touching up an image, fixing tiny flaws, and bringing items into sharper con-trast.
The Blue option can be changed from the Blue Option dialog box, as shown below.

Sharpen tool can bring up the most useful to rid the background of unwanted clutter and to deemphasize parts of the picture that you do not want viewers to notice. Sharpening tool is the exact opposite of the Blur tool. Where the Blur tool soften pixel value, the Sharpen tool hardens them and brings them into greater relief by increasing the contrast between adjecent pixel. Sharpening is best done in very high, you can end up burning the color out of an image, which probably make it look worse than it did initially.

For doing this follow the following steps:

1. Click once on the Magnifying glass to zoom in on your picture to have the magnification around 200%

2. Select the Blur tool. Choose a soft-edged brush shape from the Brush palette.

3. Double-click the Focus tools in the toolbox to open the Option palette.

4. Click the Option palette and type 5 to set the pressure to 50%.

obom b

5. Drag the Blur tool across the picture.

6. Switch to Sparpen tool by pressing Shift+R. Choose a hard edged brush. Drag it over a different part of the picture. Try to drag it along the edge of an object and not the effect.

7. Notice the Blur in first and second picture on the next page.

The Toning Tools

The Toning tolls include the Dodge, Burn, and Sponge tools, Dodge and Burn are opposites, like Sharpen and Blur, but instead of af-fecting the contrast between adjacent pixels, they either lighten or darken the area to. which the tool is applied.
Dodge and Burn Tools

Dodge, is accomplished by waving a Dodge tool, usually a cardboard circle on a wire, between the projected image from the enlarger and the photographic paper. This blocks some of the light and makes the dodge area lighter when the print is developed. Buring has the opposite effect to dodgeing-instead of lightening a small area, it darkens the area. Here by blocking the enlarger light with your hand you can reach the area to be burned.

Inside the Tools Options palette you have the 3 choices: Shadows Midtones Highlights. These option indicate the type of pixels that the tool will affect. If you want to adjust the shadows, such as marking them lighter and leaving the lighter pixels untouched, selected Shadow. The default option for the Dodge is Midtones. Selected the highlights when default option for the Dodge is Midtones. Selected the highlights when you want to lighten already lightcoloured area, leaving the darker areas untouched.

Sponge Tools

It is also a darkroom feature. When a picture in the developing tray is not turning dark enough, or looks to be underexposed or weak in colour the darkroom technician can ofter save it by sloshing some fresh, fullstrength developing chemical on a sponge and rubbing it directly on the wet paint in the tray. On a colour image, it sublety increases the colour saturation in the area to which you apply it, On a grayscale image, it increase or decreases contrast by moveing the grayscale level away from or toward midly gray.
DIFFERENT MEDIA

There are other tools which can enhance the looks of your image. One of them is the use of filter, about which we will read in the next chapter, the other are the use of various tools. One of them is Water colour. You can change any picture to its water colour counterapart.

Watercolour

For this choose Watercolour from the Filter menu and Artistic submenu. See the effect of watercolour to the following picture before and after.

You can also adjust the Brush detail Shadow intensity and Texture in the Watercolour dialog box, as shown on the next page. In the thembnail you can see the effect of the change you make.

Another effect is of Oil Painting.

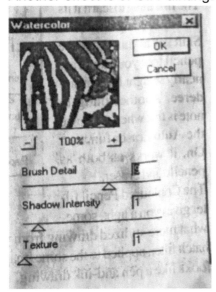

Oil Panting

All of us know the difference between watercolour and oil colour. The base is water in first whereas it is oil in the second.

For this we select the option of Underpainting from the Artistic submenu in the Filter menu.

In the dialog box, select the option shown on the next page. You can how ever differ with me and choose different option and click Ok ti see the effect as shown on the next page.

Underpainting actually builds the foundation of the main painting.

Pencil Filters

The Pencil tool has been part of every graphic pro-gram the very first ones. The first thing to learn it its that by holding down the Shift key as your drage the pencil tool you can draw nearly straight lines at any deree. Another thing to note is that when you have the Auto Eraser function On, it works as both as pencile and eraser.

The Conloured Pencil fil-ter gives you a light, some-what more stylized drawing from your original image. The cross-hatch filter, applied to the some image retains much more of the colour and details but still looks like a pen and-ink drawing.

Chalk and Charcol Filters

Since early ages Chalk and Charcoal have been used to make drawings. The same has been incorporated in Photoshop too. When you apply the Chalk and Charcol filter, Which is found on the Filter menu, you will that it reduces your pictures to three colours that you have set in the tool window. Chalk uses the background colour and Charcol becomes the foreground colour.

The Chalk and Charcol dialog box has option for both Chalk and Charkcoal area as well as the Stroke pressure option. Stroke option varies from 0 to 5 whereas the other vary from 0 to 20.

See the effect of Chalk and Charcoal and then Charcoal only given below.

USING LAYER AND MASKS:

INTRODUCTION

Layer are the various layers that you can create of the image or picture for the editing purpose and putting them one over the another for the final result. Masking is the method by which you can select a portion of the image or picture for editing and doing changes.

Layers

The Layers palette is where you control your layer. Be it be for creating, adding, delet-ing, hiding, and showing. The small versions of your images on the left of the palette are called thumbnails. Each of these small rectangles represent a separate layer.

If thumbnail are small for your liking, select the Palette Options to see more thumbnails.

CREATING A NEW LAYER

1. Using the Airbrush and your biggest brush shape, choose any light to me-dium colour and spray paint a large patch of colour on the canvas.

2. Look at the thumbnail called Background.

3. Click the small page icon at the bottom of the layer palette. You have just added a layer.

Another way of adding a new layer is by opening the menu on the right hand side of the dialog box and click at

New Layer.

A new layer like above is added.

HINDING AND SHOWING OF LAYERS

To the left of the thumbnail, you will notice small icons that resemble eyes. These indicate that a layer is visible. If you see the eye you can see the layer. If you click the eye, however, the eye disappears and the layer becomes hidden.

In the following figure Layer I is hidden and the other one is shown

WORKING WITH MULTIPLE LAYERS

Whenever you are combining two or mor image the elements you paste over the back-ground image are added on separte layer. You can use the Layer palette to control precisely how these elements are combined. You can also control the Blending modes that affect how one layer appears on top of another just as you could when painting over an image or background.

Merging Layers

The more layers you add to an image and more effect that you add to those layers, the larger your image file will become. There are two main factors here:

Merging Layers

Merging groups of layer without flattening the entire image conserves memory space but still allows you to work on the layers that you have not yet finished. Merging Down merge just the visible layers choosing the appropriate Layer, Merge commnad.

Flattening

Flattening on the other hand, compresses all visible layers down to one layer. Any layers that you have made invisible at the time of flattening lost. To flatten an image, simple choose

Layer, Flatten Image, but make sure that you are done. At this point all the layers are reduced to one.

Layer Effects

A number of automated effects that you can apply to layers, shown on the next page, are available under Layer menu and Effects submenu. They include drop shadows, glows, beveling and embossing. You can ap-ply these and see the effects.

Masks

It is the selection that you make be-cause it permits you to do something that affects only the selected area, ef-fectively masking anything that is not selected. Masks can let you change one part of a picture without changing all of it.

Quick Mask

You can mask an image in Photoshop

on your own using the Magic Wand. But it also provides with a very easy mehod too. It is called Quick mask. In this case you can see both the image and the mask at the same time. For createing a quick mask do the following:

1. You can use any selection tool to select a part of the image which you want to mask.

2. Click the Quick mask bottom in the toolbox.

3. You see a colour overly indicating the mask on the protected area, which is to say, the area not selected.

4. If the mask needs editing, select an appropriate painbrush size and from the brush palette and click the painbrush.

5. When the mask is edited to your satifaction, click at the Standard Mode button to return to the original image.
6. You can now press Ctrl+D to deselect the area and get rid of the mask from teh image.

Adding Mask to the Layer

It can be done in the following steps:

1. Open the Layer palette, if it is not already active.

2. Select teh Layer to which you want to add mask. Mask sure there are no other masks already applied to that layer.

3. To hide the entire layer, Choose Layer, Add layer Mask, Hide All.

4. To make a mask that hides or reveals a se-lected are, first make the selection on the active layer.

5. Choose Layer, Add Layer Mask, Hide Se-lection or Layer, Add layer Mask, Reveal se-lection, whichever is appropriate for your needs.

Editing layer Masks

If you click the Layer Masks thumbnail in the Layers Palette to make it active you will see the mask icon in the small square on the left of the layer thumbnail. To edit the layer, either click its thumbnail or go to the Layer menu and select Disable Layer Mask. This will put a large X through the mask to indicate that the mask is inactive.

Removing layer Mask

You can do this either by selecting layer and Removing Layer Mask or dragging the Layer mask icon in the small trash can icon the bottom of the window.

USING FILTERS:

INTRODUCTION

Filter in photoshop terminology are a set of instruction built into the program that apply specific effects to your pictures. One of them converts your image to a pattern of dots. The other one simulates flames shooting out a selected object. One of the most common problems faced in the image is that it is out of focus. It can be even fuzzy. Probably the photograph was taken by a cheap camera.

Let us discuss the various filters in details.

SHARPEN SHARPEN MORE

Sharpen and sharpen More provide different level of the same function. They work by finding areas in the image where there are significant colour changes, such as at the edged of an object. Whenever such an area is found, photoshop increases the contrast between adjacent pixels, making the lights lighter and the darks darker.

Sharpen More is the same effect as applying the Sharpen filter twice to the same picture. On the next page you will see the Original, after appling the sharpen filter and then after applying the More Sharpen filters.

BLUK FILTERS

Blur and Blur More are the two Blur filters. Blur filter is very subtle while Blur More is only a little less.

The next page will show you the effect of Blur and Blur more filter.

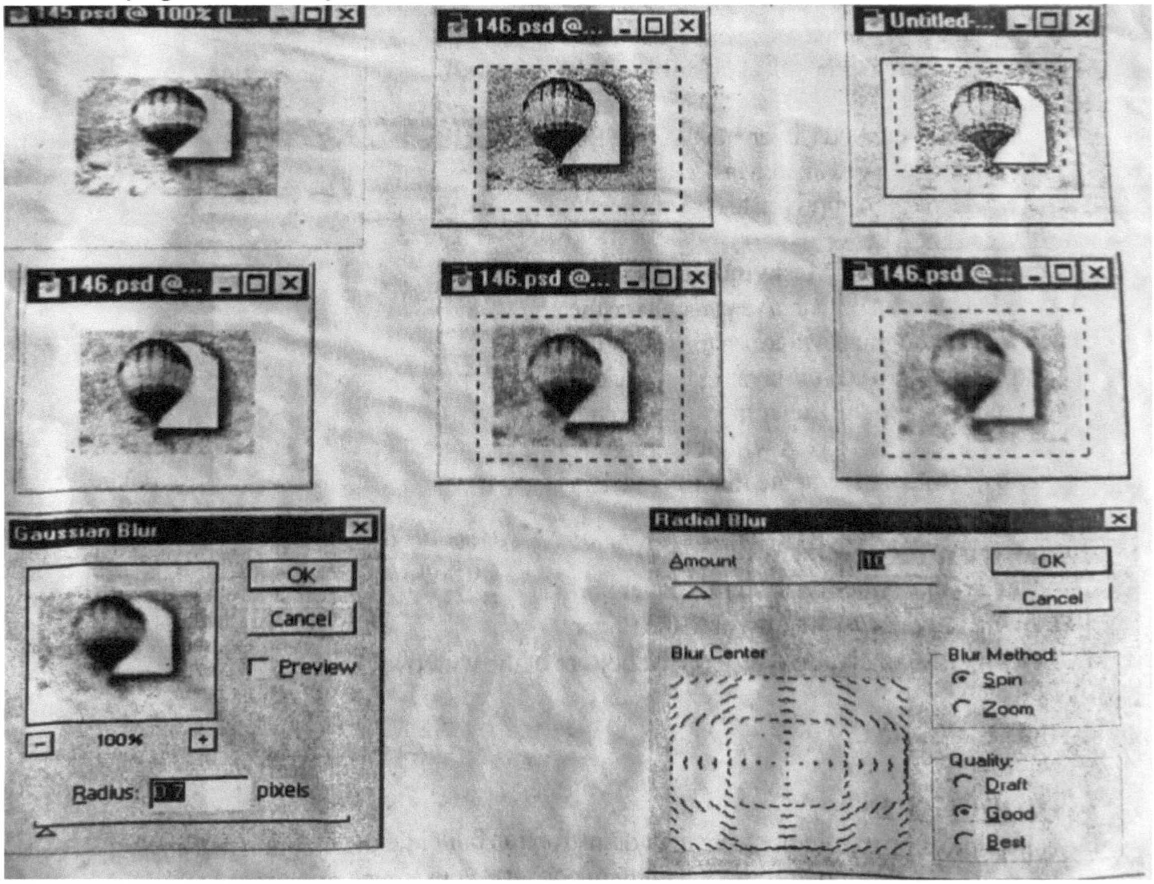

GAUSSIAN BLUR

This type of Blur is more useful since this allows you to control the blurness. It uses a mathematical formula to calculate the blurness. The Gaussian Blur dialog box lets you determine exactly how lets you determine exactly how much Blur to apply by setting a Radius value from 1 to 255.

In the following figures you see the Gaussian Blur dialog box and the picture after apply-ing this Blur.

RADIAL BLUR

The Radial Blur filter gives you 2 choices: Spin and Zoom.

Spin mode gives you a blur that looks as if the image is spining around its centre point. In the Radial Blur dialog box. You can set both an amount for the Blur effect (1-100) and a quality level (Draft, Good or Best). Zoom mode gives you the effect of zooming the effect of zooming the camera into or away from the image.

The picture after Spin effect is show below while the one with Zoom effect is shown on the next page.

Smart Blur

The Smart Blur filter is most useful for image editing and repairing. It blurs everything in the image. Smart Blur calculates the difference between colour regions to determine boundaries and it maintains these boundaries while blurring everything within them.

Smart Blur dialog box shows before and after views of the filter applied to a portrait. You can set Radius and Threshold to dertermine how much blur is applied set teh Quality to determine how the effect is calculated. The 3 models here are: normal, where Preview window shows the effect of the blurring; Edge Onloy, which shows the outlines with which Smart Blur is workiong; and Edge Overlay, which shows the outlines as black

lines on top of the image. Effect of the Normal Smart Blur is shown on the next page.

Motion Blur

It can add the appearance of motion to a stationery object by placing a directional blur for a predetermined distance. In the Montion Blur dialog box you can set both the dis-tance and direction of the blur according to how fast and in what direction you want the object to appear to be travelling.

You can apply these and see the effects.

www.ingramcontent.com/pod-product-compliance
Lightning Source LLC
LaVergne TN
LVHW060202050326
832903LV00016B/343